HOPE *and healing* AFTER SUICIDE

A practical guide for people who have lost someone to suicide in Ontario

camh
Centre for Addiction and Mental Health
Centre de toxicomanie et de santé mentale
A Pan American Health Organization / World Health Organization Collaborating Centre

Library and Archives Canada Cataloguing in Publication

Hope and healing after suicide : a practical guide for people who have lost someone to suicide in Ontario.

Issued also in French under title: L'espoir et la guérison après un suicide.
Includes bibliographical references.
Issued also in electronic formats.
ISBN 978-1-77052-346-3

1. Suicide victims--Family relationships--Ontario. 2. Bereavement-- Psychological aspects. 3. Suicide--Psychological aspects. 4. Suicide-- Ontario. I. Centre for Addiction and Mental Health

HV6548.C32O68 2011 362.2'8309713 C2011-902639-2

ISBN: 978-1-77052-346-3 (PRINT)
ISBN: 978-1-77052-347-0 (PDF)
ISBN: 978-1-77052-349-4 (ePUB)
ISBN: 978-1-77052-348-7 (HTML)

Printed in Canada

This publication may be available in other formats. For information about alternate formats or other CAMH publications, or to place an order, please contact Sales and Distribution:
Toll-free: 1 800 661-1111
Toronto: 416 595-6059
E-mail: publications@camh.net
Online store: http://store.camh.net

Website: www.camh.net

Disponible en français sous le titre : L'espoir et la guérison après un suicide : Guide pratique pour les personnes qui ont perdu un proche à la suite d'un suicide en Ontario

This guide was produced by:
Development: Margaret Kittel Canale, CAMH
Editorial: Diana Ballon, Nick Gamble, CAMH
Design: Mara Korkola, CAMH
Print production: Christine Harris, CAMH

This publication has been adapted for Ontario from the Alberta-based *Hope and Healing: A Practical Guide for Survivors of Suicide*. Permission to reproduce the publication in whole or in part has been given by the Alberta Health Services.

4080/ 07-2011/ PM089

Preface

We hope this guide has reached you at a time when it can be most helpful.

This is a practical guide to help you through...
the first few moments
then the first few hours
then the first few days
then the first few years
...after the suicide of someone close to you.

This guide—written with the help of many suicide survivors and the health professionals who work with them—focuses on the practical matters that survivors need to deal with after a suicide. We hope it will help you through this difficult time.

Please share this guide with others who may benefit from the information or who may be able to help you. To access this guide online, go to http://knowledgex.camh.net and search for "Hope and Healing after Suicide."

Contents

Acknowledgments

PROJECT LEAD

Margaret Kittel Canale, MEd, Knowledge & Innovation Support, CAMH

PROJECT TEAM

Penny Knapp, survivor of suicide

Melanie McLeod, survivor of suicide

Geri Roberts-Minialoff, program consultant, Provincial Services, CAMH

Maryann Shaw, child and adolescent psychotherapist, Department of Psychiatry, Hospital for Sick Children, Toronto

CONTRIBUTORS

Kelly Bachoo, sergeant, York Regional Police Services

A. E. Lauwers, MD, CCFP, FCFP, Deputy Chief Coroner, Investigations, Ontario

Sharon Lowe, MEd, psychotherapist

Rick Ludwig, past president, Ontario Funeral Service Association

Danette Mathias, program director, Wawa & Area Victim Services

R. S. Kane Funeral Home staff, Toronto

Duane Wenmann, sergeant, Wawa Police Service

REVIEWERS

We are indebted to the many survivors of suicide in Ontario who reviewed a draft of this book and provided feedback that enhanced the content and flow. Collectively, they lost life partners or spouses, children, parents, siblings and cousins.

We thank, too, the following Ontario reviewers whose expertise in various aspects of the content of the book ensured its completeness and accuracy:

Patrick Cusack, chartered accountant

Fran King, educational consultant and grief therapist

Kirsty Laidlaw, funeral director, Arthur Funeral Home, Sault Ste. Marie

A. E. Lauwers, MD, CCFP, FCFP, Deputy Chief Coroner, Investigations, Ontario

Irfan A. Mian, MD, FRCPC, Clinical Head, Mood and Anxiety Disorders Service, Child, Youth and Family Program, CAMH

Cathy Thompson, program consultant, Provincial Services, CAMH

Why CAMH developed this Ontario guide

This guide is an adaptation of *Hope and Healing: A Practical Guide for Survivors of Suicide*, which was developed to provide timely, practical advice to survivors of suicide in Alberta. The loss and grief experienced by family and friends—and the practical matters that need attending to—when someone dies by suicide can be especially complex and challenging.

Penny Knapp, whose son Nicholas died by suicide, approached the Centre for Addiction and Mental Health (CAMH) and asked if we could adapt the guide for Ontario. We discovered that a resource similar to the Alberta one did not exist for survivors of suicide in Ontario, so CAMH quickly said "Yes."

This Ontario version generally follows the structure of the Alberta original and contains much of the same content, with adaptations for Ontario where appropriate. With this adaptation, we've gone a step further in several ways. We've enhanced the content on mental health and grieving issues. We've included more detailed information on the practical steps to take when a family member dies. We've added more resources (such as organizations, books and websites) that survivors of suicide will find useful. And we've included the loving responses of survivors of suicide—Penny and her two daughters—as they remember a son and brother.

1

When someone close to you dies by suicide

You will survive. Yes, the grief is overwhelming. It is hard to believe now, but one hour at a time, one day at a time, you will get through it. And then, as time goes on, the pain will lessen.

What helps in the short term

Emotional reactions to a suicide are intense and overwhelming. Knowing what to expect will help you cope and begin healing.

KNOW WHAT TO EXPECT

Most survivors find it hard to think clearly. You may feel as if your brain is numb. You may forget things. You may replay the suicide over and over in your mind, and find you cannot stop asking "Why?"

You are not to blame for the choice made by another person. You are not to blame for the suicide of someone close to you.

It is not unusual to feel overwhelmed by sorrow, physically ill and angry. You may feel ashamed or guilty. Sometimes, survivors think about suicide themselves. These reactions and other strong feelings are normal. People react in different ways when they are mourning such a loss.

There is no timeline for grief. Heal at your own pace.

If you are having thoughts of harming yourself, talk to someone (for example, a friend, family member, religious or spiritual leader, or counsellor) about how to cope with your feelings and keep yourself safe.

LET OTHERS HELP YOU

Your sense of confusion is likely so great at first that it can be hard to cope—so let other people help you. Look to your friends, family, place of worship, community and others for support. They can deal with callers and help make funeral and other arrangements. They can assist you in remembering what you need to know and do and in making some decisions. They can be there to simply listen.

Telling others

WHAT TO SAY

One challenge you will face is telling others about the suicide. Although it may be difficult to speak openly about suicide, it is important to tell family and friends the truth. This allows them to help each other cope with their grief and also helps you work through yours. In some situations, you might choose to say something as brief as, "She died by suicide and I just can't talk about it yet" or "He lived with a deep depression and died by suicide." Creating a brief statement that you repeat can be helpful so that you aren't trying to think of what to say each time you need to tell someone. You do not have to disclose details to people who are not close to the family.

In addition to telling family and close friends, you will need to notify people with whom the deceased had regular contact. Because telling people can be difficult, you may want to ask someone to help you make these phone calls. The list of people to inform might include school personnel, an employer and work colleagues, doctors, religious or spiritual organizations and the owner of the property where the deceased was living.

TELLING CHILDREN AND TEENS

Tell the truth

You need to tell children and teens that the death was a suicide. While they may not need to know all the details, especially if they are very young, they do need to know that the person killed himself or herself. It may be hard to say this—but it's the truth and it's better that they hear it from you. Young people can sense when they are being lied to. And concealing the truth only fuels an atmosphere of mistrust, fear and loneliness. If you do not tell them the truth, eventually they will find out through someone else. That will be far more painful for them.

Children will ask "Why?" This is a difficult question to answer because the only person who knew why was the person who died. Make the explanation fit the age of the child. For example, a younger child can be told, "He didn't want to live anymore. He felt sad and hopeless and forgot that he could get help." Keep your answers simple and short. Children and teens will tell you what they want to know, and you need answer only what they ask about.

Show your grief

It is okay for young people to see your anger, helplessness and confusion. Observing your reactions helps them understand that their own feelings are normal and okay. Check in with them to make sure they do not take on responsibility for your feelings. They need to know it is not their job to make things better for the family. Reassure them that you and others are still able to take care of them.

Listen and reassure

Children and teens may be confused when they are told the death was a suicide. They may ask a lot of questions to make sense of the news: "Didn't he love us?" or "Why was she so sad?" Answer the questions that you can. Tell them that you do not have all the answers but that you are always there to listen. Encourage them to talk about their feelings. You may find there are times when young people benefit from talking to someone else, such as a family friend or a therapist.

Young people will need plenty of reassurance that the suicide was not their fault, that they are still loved, and that other people they care about will not die too. Emphasize that there are always other solutions to problems—so that they do not see suicide as a way of coping with their problems.

Seek help

Young people need a lot of support and comfort when a loved one dies. You may find it too difficult to support your children or reassure them when you are in the early stages of grieving. If this is the case, call on someone you trust or seek the help of a professional therapist or a bereavement support group.

Emergency response and investigation

The death of someone close to you is difficult. When the person dies by suicide, you face legal and emergency situations not typical of other deaths. The events and procedures that take place after a suicide can cause great anxiety for survivors. It may help your response to the suicide to know why various procedures are necessary.

RESPONSE TO THE EMERGENCY CALL

When a sudden death is discovered, Emergency Medical Services, the fire department and the police respond to the emergency call. When the police arrive, they notify the coroner's office of the death.

Emergency Medical Services

Emergency Medical Services (EMS) provides on-the spot medical assistance. If the person is alive, they take him or her to a hospital, where hospital staff take over his or her care. Or EMS may determine that the person has died.

Fire department

The fire department provides medical assistance to EMS, as well as extra help where needed.

Police

The police become involved in a number of ways. They provide safety for emergency personnel and other people who are present. They secure the scene. They investigate the death, and they collect identification, valuables and other items related to the person and the investigation. They may also take photographs at the site. The police may ask the person who reported the death or identified the deceased to make a statement to the police. The same may be asked of those who found or spoke to the deceased. The police will attempt to notify the next of kin. Police may also arrange for the care of pets.

The police will take control of the scene on behalf of the coroner until a post mortem is completed and the cause of death determined. This is done for your protection and the safety of others. Police will hold the scene as long as needed until released by the coroner's office.

Coroner's office

The police notify the coroner's office, who will investigate the circumstances around the death. In the case of a suicide, a coroner is the only person who can sign and issue a death certificate.

Victim assistance

The police or coroner may request (or you can request) a victim services support team to provide you with support, information and referrals. The victim services support team does their work in a confidential, caring manner 24 hours a day, seven days a week.

You may also request support and assistance from Victim Services when you are filling out forms, making funeral arrangements, attending appointments or seeking counselling services.

INVESTIGATION

An investigation is done to find out the circumstances of the suicide. This includes the identity of the person, when he or she died, where he or she died, as well as the cause and manner of death. The investigation often includes a review of the past medical history, an examination of the scene of the death and an examination of the body.

Coroner's office

The Office of the Chief Coroner investigates all unexplained and all violent deaths, including suicides, by the authority of the *Coroner's Act*. The investigation is performed by coroners who are physicians. The Office of the Chief Coroner pays the cost to transport the body from the place of death to the facility where the body will be examined by a pathologist.

You can contact the Office of the Chief Coroner in Ontario at 26 Grenville Street, Toronto ON M7A 2G9 or by calling 1 877 991-9959.

Items collected at the scene

The police retain items related to the death (including suicide notes) that are collected at the scene of the death. These items can be returned to next of kin after the investigation, but must be requested and signed for.

Police may collect and retain valuables, which will be returned to next of kin upon written request.

Autopsy

If the cause of death is obvious, an autopsy may not be done. If there is some doubt about the cause or manner of death, an autopsy may be ordered by the coroner. An autopsy may include complex laboratory tests—often results are not known for months after the death.

Consent from next of kin is not required for a pathologist's autopsy to be done. The autopsy is performed pursuant to a warrant issued by the investigating coroner. Advise the coroner if there are any cultural sensitivities or any religious or conscience-based concerns around the autopsy.

You can request a summary of the coroner's findings and the autopsy report. It can take up to nine months to receive these items.

The scene after the investigation

If the death has taken place in the home, the next of kin are responsible for cleaning up the scene. Sometimes family members choose to clean the area themselves. However, when body fluids are present, it is wise to have a certified cleaning company perform the cleaning tasks.

To identify a suitable cleaning firm, consult the telephone directory or the funeral home. Professional cleaning costs can be high but are often covered by household insurance. Contact your insurance provider for further information.

Tissue and organ donations

After a suicide, survivors may find some comfort in donating the tissues or organs of the deceased. If you wish to do this, notify the coroner. The police will tell the coroner if a donor card was found on the person.

Tissues can be donated, within certain time limits (about six to 12 hours after a death), even when death occurs outside a hospital. Whether or not organs can be donated depends on a number of factors, including the condition of the body.

Inquest

An inquest is a public hearing. The purpose of an inquest is to determine who the deceased was and how, where, when and by what means the deceased died.

An inquest can be held into deaths investigated by the coroner's office. The Office of the Chief Coroner determines which cases should go to inquest.

Holding an inquest is rare in cases of suicide. However, if the person was in custody at the time of death, holding an inquest is mandatory.

2

Working through the grief

Grief is more complicated when a death is sudden. There is no chance to say goodbye. Strong emotions arise as a result of the suicide: extreme sadness, anger, shame and guilt are normal responses to a sudden death. But you are not to blame. The search to find out why someone decided to end his or her life is a painful yet important part of working through the grief—even when there are no answers.

The stigma of suicide

You are not only grieving a loss, you are dealing with the emotions around suicide as well. Grieving a suicide can be more difficult and more complicated than grieving other deaths. There is the question of why this happened, the suddenness of the death, the means of death, and the presence of police and coroners. Although you may feel that there was something you could have done to prevent the suicide, you wouldn't feel this way if the person died from cancer, heart disease or other causes.

Many people—based on cultural, religious and societal beliefs—hold negative attitudes about death by suicide. They view suicide as a moral issue rather than as the health issue that it is. Knowing that some people feel this way, and listening to their judgmental comments, can add another element of distress on top of what you're already feeling. It may also make you want to keep the cause of death a secret.

According to the World Health Organization, 11 out of 100,000 Canadians die by suicide. This rate is higher for youth, older adults, people with mental health problems (especially depression and bipolar disorder), Aboriginal people living in northern Canada and inmates in correctional facilities. About 90 per cent of people who die by suicide have a mental health problem.

By talking about suicide, you are breaking the silence around this often unspoken topic. When you speak of suicide, use the words "died by suicide" rather than "committed suicide." The word "committed" sounds judgmental, as when we speak of "committing" a crime.

Your grief is unique

The grieving process is different for each person. Reactions to death vary according to one's personality, age, gender, culture, religious or spiritual beliefs, family background, role in the family, coping skills, relationship with the deceased, the number of losses the person has already experienced, and the circumstances of the death.

Some aspects of grief are predictable. But grief does not involve stages or phases that one passes through in a linear fashion. Rather, grief is like a roller coaster ride: it tends to ebb and flow daily and you may feel many emotions at the same time.

The hardest time can be after the most immediate or critical issues have been attended to, when there are fewer distractions, and others have returned to their daily lives. It is important for you and those who care about you to recognize that you need ongoing support.

NUMBNESS AND SHOCK

Survivors usually feel numb and in shock when they first find out about the suicide, and for several weeks after or even longer. This feeling is like sitting on the side of a play about your life, but not really taking part in life itself. Nothing seems real. The feeling of shock has a purpose—it cushions you from the pain of what has happened. Over time, the numbness fades and you will proceed with your grieving.

The grief process is different for each person.

OTHER RESPONSES

The following are some of the ways people react to the suicide of a family member or friend.

Changes in behaviours

You may find yourself acting in ways that are different from how you behaved before. This could include changes in your habits as well as changes in your relationships with others, such as:

- disturbances in your sleeping patterns
- crying—sometimes uncontrollably and for a long time
- visiting places or carrying treasured objects associated with the person who has died
- restless overactivity
- withdrawing socially (for example, by avoiding friends and phone calls)
- lack of interest in the world
- overuse of alcohol and other drugs or overdoing activities to numb the pain
- eating more or less than you usually do
- generally doing things out of character
- discovering that your usual coping mechanisms are not working for you now.

Emotional responses

Some of the emotional reactions you may experience as you grieve include:

- anger
- sadness
- guilt
- anxiety
- shock
- denial
- helplessness
- hopelessness
- apathy
- despair

- numbness
- relief (sometimes, if the person was ill for a long time)
- yearning or pining for the person
- frustration
- irritability
- loneliness or isolation
- feeling overwhelmed.

Spiritual responses

Your world view may shift as a result of the death. You could find yourself, for example:

- questioning your spiritual or religious beliefs, and other values
- searching for meaning to understand why the death occurred
- reconstructing how you understand death
- losing a fear of death
- feeling you are being punished
- visiting mediums to communicate with the deceased
- performing rituals to keep alive your connection with the deceased
- feeling an increased sense of helplessness due to the sudden and traumatic death.

Cognitive or mental responses

Your thoughts, perceptions, reasoning skills and intuition may change. For example, you may find yourself:

- being preoccupied, and even obsessed, with thoughts of the deceased
- sensing the dead person's presence
- disbelieving or denying what has happened
- feeling disconnected from reality
- being distracted
- being unable to concentrate

- being forgetful
- being unable to think straight
- lacking the ability to make decisions
- looking for signs that the person is there.

Physical responses

You may find that your body works differently or that you experience physical symptoms that are not normal for you. This could include:

- being clumsy and unco-ordinated
- lacking energy or feeling extremely tired
- being hyper-alert and unable to rest
- muscle weakness
- difficulty breathing
- tightness in the chest or chest pain
- dry mouth or problems swallowing
- feeling emptiness in the stomach
- nausea or digestive upsets
- irregular heartbeat
- sensitivity to noise
- startling easily
- changes in appetite
- frequent colds and other illnesses.

GRIEVING TAKES TIME

How long people grieve varies. Occasionally survivors get stuck as they work through their grief. If this happens, a therapist can help. You need people in your life who can support you.

Clinical depression is different from normal grief in that it is more intense and prolonged. If you are concerned about depression, please contact your doctor.

Young people and grief

WHEN CHILDREN GRIEVE

Children do not show their feelings in the same way adults do. You may see their emotions expressed in their behaviour and play. And they may talk about their feelings with other children rather than with adults.

Sometimes children look as though they have not been affected by the death. They may cry for a while and then return to play and within moments be laughing—this is because their words and behaviour do not always reflect how they feel inside. Adults often misinterpret this behaviour as a lack of capacity to grieve; however, what adults are observing is the child mourning in manageable chunks.

It is common for children, as they grow, to grieve the loss of a loved family member at a later time. They may develop new feelings and new responses to the death, even years after the suicide. They often ask different questions as they try to understand what happened from a more mature point of view. And they may experience grief again as they pass through various developmental events, such as graduations, proms, getting their first job, getting married and the birth of their first child.

Children need to deal with their grief. Be available to talk with them about the death, or have them talk to someone else they and you trust.

Signs of children's grief

Like adults, the ways in which children express their grief varies from child to child. The following signs may indicate that a

child is mourning the death:
- questions; for example, about why the person died and when they are coming back
- regressive behaviour, such as thumb sucking
- fear of separation from a surviving parent or other important people in their lives
- clingy behaviour
- anger, such as having temper tantrums or being non-compliant
- physical problems, such as loss of appetite, nightmares and having trouble sleeping
- anxiety about school: this could appear as irritability, withdrawal or difficulty concentrating and may be interpreted as behavioural problems.

Developmental stages and perceptions of death

The age of a child at the time of the death will affect how he or she responds to it.

FOUR YEARS AND YOUNGER

Children at this age may not understand the differences between life and death. Children who are four and under:
- often think in concrete terms
- may associate death with sleep
- may not see death as final
- engage in "magical thinking"; for example, children do not have a sense of permanence: they believe the deceased person can return or that they can visit the deceased.

AROUND FIVE TO EIGHT YEARS

Children at this age are learning to see death as final for all living things, including themselves. They may:
- ask many questions

- be curious about what happens to the body
- engage in magical thinking—this could show up as thought processes indicating the child thinks he or she caused the death or fears that death is contagious.

AROUND NINE TO 12 YEARS

Children in the preteen years of nine to 12:

- realize that death can happen to anyone, whether they are young or old
- may continue to believe they are invincible
- understand that memories keep the person alive.

WHEN TEENS GRIEVE

Teens experiencing the suicide of a family member or friend may be confronting death for the first time. The teen years are marked by many firsts which is why, at times, teens seem to have dramatic reactions to life events. As with all firsts, teens don't have prior experience to draw on and are unsure about what to do with their grief. They grieve differently than adults and, because their brains are still developing, problem solving may not be a well-developed skill.

Teen mourning rituals tend to be more collaborative and less private than adults'. They may exhibit more anger and feel guilty about not knowing about the risk of suicide or doing something to prevent it. Like adults, they will ask why and try to comprehend how someone can end his or her life. At the same time, they may be acutely aware of their own self-destructive patterns.

Peer groups and other groups they may belong to (such as clubs, teams, and cultural and religious groups) can be helpful to teens. Expressing themselves through technology is common with teens and can also be useful in the grieving process (for example, writing an online journal or blog as a way to remember and celebrate the person).

Signs of teens' grief

As with adults and younger children, the ways in which adolescents express their grief will vary from teen to teen. Some common signs of teen grief include:

- appearing confused, depressed, angry or guilty
- experiencing physical complaints, such as having difficulty eating or sleeping
- masking their hurt and pain to fit in with their peers
- changes in school work patterns, either by burying themselves in school work and doing well or by not being able to concentrate and doing poorly
- feeling different or that they no longer fit in with their peer group
- relying on friends or changing to other groups who they feel understand them more
- becoming more responsible and taking on the roles and responsibilities of the deceased (especially if the deceased was their parent), or being more helpful to their parents or the surviving parent
- becoming overly concerned with the safety of family members and friends
- feeling like they have lost their family because the dynamics have shifted.

Developmental stage and perceptions of death

Most adolescents understand that everyone will die, but feel distant from the fact that death can happen to them.

WAYS TO HELP YOUNG PEOPLE COPE WITH GRIEF

For young people, the seriousness of the loss takes them beyond the innocence of childhood. Their world is shattered. Their once-predictable life has become uncertain and frightening. Yet grieving children and teens are amazingly resilient and, with support from loved ones, can grieve and begin healing. Children and teens need this support, regardless of how they seem to be coping. Demonstrations of love and ongoing support are the greatest gifts you can give a grieving child or teen. If you are also grieving, make sure that you have your own supports, while also supporting your children.

There are many ways you can help children and teens cope with the death and their ensuing grief. Here are some suggestions.

Talking about the death

- Be "present" and focused and listen to what they are saying—and what they are not saying.
- Do not force young people to talk about the death. Wait until they are ready.
- Create a loving and safe environment where young people can ask questions.
- Answer questions. If young people do not get their questions answered, they fill in the blanks and use their imaginations to come up with scenarios that are often worse.
- Respond only to what the young person is asking about. Do not provide more information than asked for.
- Accurately describe what has occurred with concepts and words the young person can understand. For example, do not say "Auntie is sleeping"; instead, you could say "Auntie was

sick and chose to make her body stop working."

- Encourage children and teens to express their thoughts, feelings and fears. Help them to identify these feelings.
- Make sure young people know it is okay to feel happy as well as sad. Feeling happy (or feeling better) does not mean that they are not sad about the death or that they have forgotten the person.

Keeping up routines

- Provide consistency and routines for children and teens.
- Engage young people in activities that can take their minds off what has happened or can help them celebrate the person's life. This could include drawing, moulding clay, writing, playing with toys, making a memory picture book or a memory box with favourite mementos, framing a picture of the person, planting a tree or garden in the person's honour, lighting a memorial candle or visiting the cemetery.

What helps healing

IT WILL GET BETTER

Healing does not mean forgetting. It means that the sadness and other feelings do not get in the way of your life as much as they did in the beginning. You will heal and the pain will lessen.

Keep on talking

Some survivors seek out information about suicide and grieving; others choose not to do so. Many survivors say they talked their way through their grief. As you heal, talk about your memories of the person who died by suicide. Find a safe person, or several people, who will let you talk and are comfortable hearing about your pain. The people you choose to talk to may or may not have experienced the suicide with you.

When you are open about the suicide, you give others permission to talk about it too. Keeping the suicide a secret adds to the feeling of shame. A lot more people than you realize have been touched by suicide.

At times you may need to be distracted from your grieving. That is okay. Do not feel guilty about losing yourself in something else for a while.

Hold on to your memories

Often survivors, both adults and young people, have found comfort in holding on to items that remind them of the person, such as furniture, clothing, jewellery or favourite objects. You might like to put together an album with photos of the deceased. You can also build a collection of memories by asking other people to tell you their stories of the deceased and recording them in a notebook.

Do what works for you

Sometimes friends and family want to help but they do not know what to do. They may feel uncomfortable talking about suicide because of the stigma attached to it. They may be worried that you or others will cry when they bring up the subject. They might act strangely and not mention the suicide at all. Do not let this get in the way of your talking about it when you need to. Tell people it is okay to mention the suicide and let them know they can help you by simply listening. Most people really do care.

Choose to do what feels right for you, not what pleases other people. It is okay to say "No" when invited to do something you do not feel ready to do.

LATER REACTIONS

Some survivors feel even more pain and emptiness several months after the death. The tasks of planning the funeral and dealing with financial and legal matters have been completed. Friends and family have offered their sympathy and then needed to get back to their lives. Be prepared for this and reach out for help when you need it.

Difficult days

There will be many times throughout the years when coping with the loss becomes more difficult, such as the anniversary of the death, birthdays and holidays. These occasions can intensify your grief—and you may feel more on edge in the days or weeks leading up to them. It will help you to plan ahead and talk to other family members about how they want to spend the day. This gives everyone a chance to support each other and talk about their grief.

Often the anxiety about the date is more intense leading up to the day than on the actual day. Developing rituals to mark important days can be helpful. The ritual can be repeated each year or changed and modified as time passes.

There are many other difficult situations that we cannot predict. These include receiving mail or a phone call for the person or running into someone who does not know about the death. Anticipating these events with a practised statement or an already composed letter or e-mail can be helpful.

Finding the answers

You may never know the answer to "Why?" Many times survivors identify what they consider to be a triggering event, such as a relationship breakup, as the "cause" of the suicide when, in most cases, the person had been in extreme emotional or physical pain for a long time. As you work through your grief, you will gradually learn to live with questions that cannot be answered.

SUPPORT GROUPS

You may find it helpful to talk to other survivors of suicide. The healing power of a shared experience is strong and talking to others who have lost someone to suicide can help you work through your own grief. Sharing your experience can help break your sense of isolation and give you a sense that you are not alone in your journey.

There are many bereavement groups available, through numerous organizations. You may find it most helpful to join a group that is specific to your loss (for example, a spouse, a child, a sibling) and that is with other survivors of suicide.

You may also find it useful to seek support among people and groups who share the same spiritual, religious or cultural world view as you and who can better relate to your experience of death and suicide. Aboriginal people, for example, may find comfort in talking to an elder or attending a sweat lodge or talking circle.

For further help and information, see Chapter 5, "Resources."

PROFESSIONAL THERAPISTS

Grieving is a normal, healthy response to a significant loss in your life. Seeking help from a therapist can provide guidance and offer some understanding of your difficult journey. A professional can also dispel some of the myths associated with grieving and help you assess the need for medication.

For help in finding a therapist, see "Professional therapists" in Chapter 5, "Resources."

LOOKING AFTER YOURSELF

For now...

Grieving takes energy, so forgive yourself when you simply can't do the things you think you "should" do. In the beginning, your grief journey may use up all the energy you need just to get through the day, especially if you have to care for others or deal with some of the practical matters discussed earlier.

The more you take care of yourself, the better equipped you will be to get through each day. Each person is unique. What works for one person may not be helpful to another person. And there may be days when you find that doing the same thing that was helpful yesterday may not be as helpful today. Here are some suggestions that may help:

- Make time for you. Use your alone time to think, plan, meditate, pray, journal, remember and mourn.
- Surround yourself with safe people and safe places to support you on this difficult journey.
- Accept help. Do not be afraid to tell people what you need. Often, people may not know what to say or how to help

unless they are told directly. For example, you could suggest tasks (such as mowing the grass, shopping for groceries or going for a walk with you) to friends and family who want to help. You could create a venue, such as a blog, where you could tell people how they can help.

One day...

As time passes, you will find the courage and resources to keep going and have the energy to be more purposeful about taking care of yourself. Here are some suggestions:

- Manage your health. Eat a balanced diet and get physical exercise. Drink plenty of water and avoid or limit your use of alcohol, caffeine and tobacco. Check out the Public Health Agency of Canada at www.phac-aspc.gc.ca for more information on all aspects of your health.
- Keep a journal. Record your thoughts, feelings, hopes and dreams. Writing them down may help make them more real. Using technology (such as e-mail and Facebook) is one way to keep in touch with people.
- Talk things out. Confide in a trusted friend, family member, colleague, religious or spiritual leader, or professional therapist.
- Practise relaxation techniques such as deep breathing and visualization.
- Use music, art or other creative therapies to explore and work through your feelings.
- Read about suicide, grief and the ways in which people have used their spirituality to cope in times of tragedy. Sources of information include your local library, bookstores, the Internet, funeral homes, community agencies and places of worship. For suggested readings, see Chapter 5, "Resources."
- Create a list of resources. Include the people and organizations that can help you and your family when things are not going well.

- Take a break from your grief. See a movie, visit a museum or art gallery, pursue a hobby or go for a walk with a friend.
- Re-establish a routine in your life. Survivors often find the structure and distraction of returning to work or getting a new routine helpful.
- Give back to your community. Many survivors have found a sense of peace and fulfillment in shared compassion and in using their experiences to help others.
- Take small steps. Recognize each step forward and reward yourself in some way.

Whatever you do, make sure it feels right to you.

3

Practical matters

A funeral is an important ritual that gives family and friends a chance to reflect and grieve while being supported by others who care. It allows them to say goodbye and begin accepting the reality of the loss.

Arranging a funeral

Before organizing a funeral, survivors will need to determine who is legally responsible for making funeral arrangements. Many people have complicated relationships with the deceased, so it may not be clear who has the final say.

You may find it useful to appoint a family representative—someone who is a clear thinker, has a vision of what needs to happen and has the respect of most of the family members. This person could be a distant relative or a close family friend. It is not this person's role to make decisions; rather, he or she would accompany the family to the funeral home and help the family make decisions that make sense.

Friends, family, clergy or the funeral director can help you decide what type of funeral arrangements to make. Honour the wishes of the deceased as much as possible if he or she had communicated them to you or others. The deceased may have made burial arrangements, left written instructions about the use of his or her body parts, or talked to you or other family members or friends about what he or she wanted to happen upon death.

Guidelines and customs for funeral services vary. Different cultures, religions and spiritual groups have special rituals to recognize a death.

To choose a funeral home, ask for suggestions from family, friends, and spiritual or religious leaders, or check local listings in a phone book. You might want to meet with staff from more than one funeral home so you can find the one that best suits your needs in terms of hospitality, services and facilities available, and costs.

FUNERAL SERVICE AND BURIAL OR CREMATION

A funeral allows family and friends to say goodbye and begin accepting the reality of the loss. The funeral and associated rituals are for the benefit of those left behind, and are an important part of the healing process.

The funeral service or ceremony is often held in a place of worship or a funeral home chapel. However, it is up to the family to decide what kind of ceremony they want and where it will be held. If you are having difficulty making decisions at this time, rely on someone you trust to help you.

You can decide whether the service will be public or private. If the deceased's spiritual or religious practices or cultural background lay out guidelines to be followed upon death, you will likely want to follow them.

A committal service is a brief service where final words of farewell are spoken. It happens at the end of the traditional service and may be done at the graveside, crematorium or religious institution.

In a military service, the deceased is given military honours. This is available to any veteran or serving member of Canada's Armed Forces.

A memorial service is similar to a funeral service, except the body of the deceased is not present.

If you choose to not have a service, you can ask a funeral home to care for the body by arranging for burial or cremation.

Often the family sets aside time for visitation (for example, at the funeral home in the days prior to the funeral service or in the home in the days following the service). The visitation period can be an important part of the healing journey, as family and friends visit and offer comfort.

TAKING CHILDREN TO THE FUNERAL

Encourage children to take part in the funeral or ceremony because it helps them as their grief unfolds. It is wise to talk with children ahead of time—in a way that they can understand—about what will happen at the funeral and what behaviour is expected of them. On the other hand, if children do not want to attend the funeral, assure them that it is okay not to be there and help them grieve in their own way.

Offer children a role in planning the funeral and allow them at least minor choices (for example, what to wear to the service or whether to bring a flower to place on the casket). Children must be allowed to change their mind about choices they have made (such as attending the ceremony), even at the last moment.

TALKING ABOUT SUICIDE AT THE FUNERAL

It is okay to talk about the suicide at the funeral service. Make sure any mention of suicide in the service is done without judgment. It may be appropriate to acknowledge the pain the deceased was feeling. Although it is difficult to talk about the suicide, it is generally more difficult to spend all your energy covering up or hiding the cause of death. In general, you will find people deeply respectful of your hurt and not prying with their questions.

Celebrate the life of your loved one and talk about memories. Some survivors have found it helpful to place an open notebook on a table at the funeral and encourage others to write down their memories of the deceased. Allow yourself to grieve the relationship you shared. Funerals are for the living—to acknowledge that a valuable life has been lived and that the end of that life has a deep impact on the people left behind.

DEATH NOTIFICATION

Writing an obituary is a difficult task. Some families feel comfortable with being open and frank, others do not. Funeral home staff can help you prepare the obituary. Spiritual and religious leaders may help you find the appropriate words. Choose wording that does not perpetuate the stigma of suicide.

FUNERAL COSTS

Funeral homes are required to provide a full listing of funeral services and merchandise prices without cost or obligation to allow you to assess the total cost prior to making any funeral agreements. The average cost of a traditional funeral in Ontario is between $7,000 and $10,000. This amount can be less, depending on the services required and the related merchandise selected.

Many families rely on the deceased's life insurance to help cover costs, although death by suicide often has an impact on a life insurance claim. An insurance broker should be able to help you with the policy claim.

Other sources of financial help include the Canada Pension Plan death benefit; Veterans Affairs (for war veterans or members of the Canadian Armed Forces); band councils or Indian and Northern Affairs Canada (for status Indians); work-related benefits programs; and your local social services department, if you already receive assistance or can't pay funeral costs. Often, the funeral home has the resources available to assist you in completing the necessary forms when seeking financial help, or will contact the social service department for you.

For further information on financial resources, see "Financial Matters" on page 39 and "Benefits" on page 48 later in this chapter.

Dealing with personal, legal and financial matters

You need to deal with a number of legal and financial matters after a death. You may want to ask other family members or close friends to help you with some of these matters during this difficult time.

Some funeral homes will do some of the work for you by notifying government offices of the death. This could include handling documents related to social insurance numbers, health cards, passports and the Canada Pension Plan.

You increase the likelihood of making wise choices when you seek the advice of professionals before making any major decisions that may affect your legal, financial or personal situation.

FIRST STEP: GATHER DOCUMENTS

The first step in dealing with financial matters is to gather the deceased's documents. This must be done before you (or your financial advisor or the executor of the will) can take care of matters related to the estate. Set up a folder to keep all the personal documents and records of legal and financial matters together.

NEXT STEPS: TAKE APPROPRIATE ACTIONS

Once all documents have been gathered, you will have to cancel, transfer and apply for various financial benefits or obligations. There are fees associated with some of these matters.

In this section, you will find lists of the most common items to address, under the following headings: personal documents, the estate, health care, financial matters, legal matters, property, memberships, benefits and your estate planning.

Personal documents

Below is a list of personal documents that it is good to have available in case you are asked for them.

❑ Death certificate

You must have the death certificate before you can cancel or transfer things registered to the deceased and before you can apply for benefits. For some transactions, you will need to provide certified copies of the death certificate; in other cases, a regular copy will be accepted.

If the funeral home does not provide them or if you need additional copies, you can obtain certified copies of the death certificate at www.serviceontario.ca or by calling 1 800 461-2156.

❑ Birth certificate

❑ Indian status card

This card is also known as the Certificate of Indian Status.

❑ Driver's licence

You can cancel a driver's licence and obtain a refund for the unused portion of the fee at any Ministry of Transportation office.

At the office, you will fill out an application for refund form and submit it with the driver's licence and copy of the death certificate. You can call the Ministry of Transportation at 1 800 387-3445 for more information.

❑ Marriage certificate

❑ Passport

If the deceased held a valid passport at the time of death, you can make it null and void by diagonally cutting off the top right-hand corner.

Or you could mail the passport, along with a copy of the death certificate, to Passport Office, Department of Foreign Affairs and International Trade, Ottawa ON K1A 0G3. The Passport Office will take the passport out of service. If you would like to keep the passport as a keepsake, you can ask for it to be returned to you.

❑ The will

Refer to "The Estate" on the next page.

❑ Social insurance number

Cancel the deceased's social insurance number.

You can do this by sending the card, along with a copy of the death certificate, to Social Insurance Number Registration, Box 7000, Bathurst NB E2A 1A2. Or you can take the card to the Human Resources and Skills Development Canada office in your area. The phone number is 1 800 206-7218.

The estate

Disposing of a deceased person's assets is usually done through a will. A will is a written record that details how a person's belongings, or estate, will be divided upon death. The executor is responsible for taking care of the estate and should be notified as soon as possible after the death.

If you do not know if the deceased had a will or where to find it, you may have to search for the last signed and dated will. Places to look include the person's home, safety deposit box or with his or her lawyer.

IF THERE IS A WILL

Probating a will occurs when a court of law proves that the will is valid. If the estate is small or held jointly, there may be no need for probate. Any property held jointly (such as real estate, bank accounts and bonds) can be easily transferred to the surviving spouse or individual named. A bank may require probate if there is a large amount of money that is not held jointly, or for other reasons.

IF THERE IS A HANDWRITTEN NOTE

Sometimes a signed, handwritten note that distributes a person's property and possessions may be used as a will. This includes suicide notes; however, suicide notes might be challenged in a court of law, on the grounds of mental incapacitation. Contact your lawyer for more information.

IF THERE IS NO WILL OR YOUR SITUATION IS COMPLICATED

The Office of the Public Guardian and Trustee will protect the interests of potential beneficiaries if an Ontario resident dies and leaves an estate, and there is no one to administer it.

If your situation is complicated for other reasons, such as marital separation or common-law relationships, you may need to contact a lawyer.

For more information on wills, powers of attorney, and the Office of the Public Guardian and Trustee, contact the Ministry of the Attorney General at 1 800 518-7901 or go to www.attorneygeneral.jus.gov.on.ca.

Health care

- ❑ **Ontario Health Insurance Plan**

  Cancel the deceased's Ontario Health Insurance Plan (OHIP) coverage.

  You will need a "Change of Information" form that you can obtain at www.health.gov.on.ca. Mail the completed form, the death certificate and the health card (cut in half) to Ministry of Health and Long-Term Care, PO Box 48, Kingston ON K7L 5J3. Or you can contact Service Ontario at 1 800 268-1154 for assistance with this process.

- ❑ **Supplemental health insurance**

  If the deceased had additional health insurance coverage, such as Ontario Blue Cross, notify the insurance provider and cancel the coverage.

- ❑ **Prescription drugs**

  Contact the pharmacy to close the deceased's file. Some pharmacies give refunds for unused, unopened medications.

❑ **Health care providers**
Notify doctors, dentists and other health care providers of the death.

Financial matters

You will need to identify the deceased's assets and liabilities (including debts).

❑ **Bank accounts**
Contact all financial institutions (for example, banks, trust companies and credit unions) where the deceased had chequing or savings accounts, and inform them of the death. Ask the issuing banks to cancel bank cards held by the deceased.

Any accounts held in common (joint accounts) can be transferred to the survivor. You will need to speak to your financial advisor or the bank holding these accounts for specific information on how to transfer the accounts.

If you require information on unclaimed bank balances, call the Bank of Canada at 1 888 891-6398.

❑ **Safety deposit box**
Make an appointment with the bank manager to review the contents of the deceased's safety deposit box.

❑ **Credit cards**
Contact the issuing institutions (such as banks and stores) to cancel credit cards held by the deceased. Most credit cards have a 1 800 number on the back. For joint-signature credit cards, you will have to send them the death certificate to cancel the deceased's signature.

- [ ] **Investments**

  Ask your financial advisor or bank for information on how to transfer these assets (for example, stocks, bonds, GICs and RRSPs).

- [ ] **Canada Savings Bonds**

  Cancel or redeem Canada Savings Bonds held in the deceased's name.

  For information on transferring or redeeming Canada Savings Bonds held by someone who has died, call 1 800 575-5151 or visit csb.gc.ca.

- [ ] **Canada Pension Plan benefits**

  Cancel Canada Pension Plan (CPP) benefits. The estate is entitled to the CPP cheque in the month in which the death occurred.

  Notify Service Canada of the death at 1 800 277-9914 or by mail to one of the Ontario regional offices. For more information, call the 1 800 number or go to www.servicecanada.gc.ca.

- [ ] **Old Age Security benefits**

  Cancel Old Age Security benefits. The estate is entitled to the pension cheque in the month in which the death occurred.

  Notify Service Canada of the death at 1 800 277-9914 or by mail to one of the Ontario regional offices. For more information, call the 1 800 number or go to www.servicecanada.gc.ca.

❑ **International benefits plans**

If the deceased was receiving benefits from other countries, notify the relevant agency of the death so they can cancel payments and provide benefits to survivors, if applicable.

❑ **Veterans services benefits**

If the deceased was receiving benefits from Veterans Affairs Canada, notify them of the death.

For more information, call 1 866 522-2122 or go to www.vac-acc.gc.ca.

❑ **Social assistance**

Cancel benefits received through Ontario Works and the Ontario Disability Support Program.

For more information, call ServiceOntario at 1 800 267-8097.

❑ **Life insurance**

Notify life insurance companies of the death and inquire about payouts. The deceased may have had more than one type of insurance policy (for example, personal insurance and a policy through his or her workplace).

In Canada, most life insurance policies must have been held for at least 24 months to be valid if the death is by suicide. (Check the policy to see if there are exclusions.) There may also be special circumstances where a policy held for less than 24 months can be challenged in court by the family of someone who died by suicide. Consult a lawyer or the insurance provider for more information.

- **Mortgage life insurance**
  If the deceased held mortgage life insurance (not the same as mortgage insurance), the mortgage will be paid upon death. The mortgage company will require a copy of the death certificate. Some policies will not cover deaths by suicide if they occur within two years of the start of coverage. Review the policy or consult with the bank for specific details.

- **Loan agreements**
  You need to address individual or co-signed loans from banks or other institutions. These may or may not be insured.

  You also need to address personal loans (monies owed or owing) between the deceased and other individuals.

- **Lease and rental contracts**
  Cancel lease and rental contracts in the name of the deceased, or transfer them to another name.

- **Spousal and child support agreements**
  If the deceased was paying spousal (alimony) or child support, you will want to find out if any monies are due to the recipients.

  For more information, contact the Family Responsibility Office at 1 800 267-4330 (live agent) or 1 800 267-7263 (automated service) or go to www.justice.gc.ca.

- **Funeral costs**
  Take final invoices (for example, from the funeral home) and a funeral director's proof of death, or the death certificate, to a bank manager. Most financial institutions will draw up a bank draft from the deceased's account to pay for all funeral-

related expenses. The bank will make out the drafts to the companies named on the invoices.

- ❑ **Estate account**

  You may need to open an estate account to protect estate funds. Seek advice on this matter from reputable legal sources and advisors.

- ❑ **Income taxes**

  A final income tax return must be filed for the deceased.

  If the death occurred between January 1 and October 31, the final T-1 return is due by April 30 of the next year. If the death occurred between November 1 and December 31, the final T-1 return is due six months after the death. If tax returns from previous years have not been completed, they must also be filed. If an estate trust must be established, a T-3 tax return must be filed for each year of the life of the estate trust.

  You may want to get a clearance certificate before you distribute any property under your control. A clearance certificate certifies that all amounts for which the deceased is liable to the Canada Revenue Agency have been paid, or that security has been accepted for the payment. If you do not get a certificate, you can be liable for any amount the deceased owes.

  For more information and to obtain the necessary forms, contact the Canada Revenue Agency at 1 800 959-8281 or go to www.cra-arc.gc.ca.

- ❑ GST/HST credit

  GST/HST credits are paid quarterly in July, October, January and April.

  If the deceased received the GST/HST credit, his or her spouse or common-law partner may be eligible to receive the credit based on his or her net income. If the deceased was a child receiving the credit, payments stop the quarter after the child's date of death.

  For more information on the GST/HST credit (including cancelling payments, returning payments and eligibility for the credit), contact the Canada Revenue Agency at 1 800 959-8281 or go to www.cra-arc.gc.ca.

- ❑ Rewards programs

  If the deceased was a member of rewards programs (such as Air Miles, Aeroplan, HBC and Shopper's Optimum), check if you can transfer the points to someone else.

- ❑ Debts

  The person who administers the estate is responsible for paying bills from the estate for monies the deceased person owed. This could include balances owing on credit cards, medical accounts, insurance and car payments.

Legal matters

You may need to consult with a lawyer regarding various aspects of the deceased's estate, such as disposing of assets (see "The Estate" on page 37) and property-related matters.

- [ ] Probate

  Probating may be necessary or preferable for some estates and not for others. Consult with a lawyer about the need to probate the deceased's estate.

- [ ] Lawsuits

  If the deceased had outstanding judgments for or against him or her, the estate may need to settle them.

Property

PERSONAL POSSESSIONS

The deceased's will may designate beneficiaries for personal possessions such as jewellery, art and household items. If the will does not mention who is to receive specific items, family members may find it comforting to keep some possessions as a remembrance.

HOUSING

- [ ] Land titles

  If the deceased owned real estate (such as a house, condominium or cottage) and designated a beneficiary in his or her will, the property will have to be transferred to the beneficiary. Contact a lawyer to update the deed to the land and to check if there are any liens (legal claims or holds) on the property that may prevent its immediate transfer or sale.

- [ ] Mortgage

  Advise the mortgage holder of the death.

- [ ] Rental property

  If the deceased lived in a rental property, terminate the lease if possible. If you are not able to terminate the lease, you may want to sublet the property for the duration of the lease.

- ❑ **Utility accounts**

  Cancel or transfer utility accounts, such as telephone, cable TV, water, electricity, gas and the Internet. For example, if your household utility bills were in the name of the deceased, transfer them to a new name. Contact each utility company for information on how to do this.

- ❑ **Home insurance**

  Cancel or transfer home insurance policies on properties owned by the deceased.

- ❑ **Canada Post**

  Canada Post will redirect mail from the deceased's last known address. Canada Post provides this service for one year at no charge.

  You need to apply for this service in person at a post office. You will need a copy of the death certificate and proof that you are the deceased's legal representative. For more information, you can call 1 800 267-1177 or go to www.canadapost.ca.

VEHICLES

- ❑ **Vehicle registrations**

  If the deceased had vehicles registered in his or her name, the ownership of these vehicles will need to be transferred. Before doing anything, you will want to check if there is a lien on the vehicle or a will directing disposition of the vehicle. A probate registry agent can help you do this.

  If a living spouse wants to transfer the deceased's vehicle to his or her name, the spouse must go to a Ministry of Transportation office with a copy of the death certificate, the will and proof of ownership as well as personal identification.

To transfer the vehicle to a close family member, the vehicle must first be transferred to the living spouse. The living spouse can then transfer the vehicle as a tax-free gift to another qualifying family member. For more information about transferring or selling a vehicle, contact the Ministry of Transportation at 1 800 387-3445 or go to www.mto.gov.on.ca.

❑ Vehicle insurance

Cancel or transfer insurance on vehicles owned by the deceased.

❑ Driver's licence

If the deceased had a valid driver's licence, you can apply for a refund on the unused portion of the licence when you notify the Ontario licensing authority.

For more information, contact the Ministry of Transportation at 1 800 387-3445 or go to www.mto.gov.on.ca.

❑ Accessible parking permit

To cancel an accessible parking permit (previously called a disability parking permit), take or send the permit—along with a copy of the death certificate or a note explaining the reason for cancellation—to a licensing office of the Ministry of Transportation.

Go to the Ministry of Transportation website at www.mto.gov.on.ca to locate local licencing offices.

Memberships

The deceased may have held memberships in various organizations, such as sports or recreation clubs, professional associations and libraries. Cancel the memberships, or transfer them to another name if appropriate.

Benefits

When someone dies, various benefits are paid to the estate or designated beneficiaries.

❑ **Employer benefits**
Contact the employer to report the death, collect the final pay cheque, discuss where to send the T4 slip, and determine if there are benefits owing. Benefits could include group life insurance proceeds, commissions, bonuses, pension plan benefits, and compensation for unused vacation days and sick leave.

❑ **Employment insurance**
If the person was receiving employment insurance benefits at the time of death, benefits up to and including the day of the death may be owed to the deceased and will be paid to a legal representative or beneficiary.

For more information, call 1 800 206-7218 or go to www.servicecanada.gc.ca.

❑ **Canada Pension Plan survivor benefits**
The Canada Pension Plan (CPP) provides three types of survivor benefits: a death benefit, survivor's pension and children's benefit.

A **CPP death benefit** is a one-time payment made to the estate of the deceased contributor, a surviving spouse, a common-law partner or other next of kin.

A **CPP survivor's pension** will be paid to the deceased's spouse or common-law partner. Legally separated spouses may also qualify for this benefit if the deceased did not have a cohabiting common-law partner. Same-sex common-law partners may also be eligible for this benefit. The amount of the benefit awarded will depend on the age of the survivor and other dependency factors.

A **CPP children's benefit** may be paid to natural or adopted dependent children of the deceased contributor, or children in the care and control of the contributor at the time of death. To qualify for this benefit, children must be 17 years of age or under; or 18 to 25 years of age and attending school or university full-time.

To find out if you are eligible and to apply for these CPP benefits, call 1 800 277-9914 or go to www.servicecanada.gc.ca. Apply as soon as possible after the death to ensure you get the full benefits you are eligible for. You will need to supply various documents, including a copy of the death certificate.

❑ Allowance for the Survivor program
This program provides a monthly non-taxable benefit to low-income widowed spouses who are not yet eligible for the Old Age Security pension and who are aged 60 to 64. This benefit is payable to someone who, at the time of death, was married to the deceased or living common law (including in a same-sex relationship).

At age 65, most people receiving this benefit will automatically have it changed to the Old Age Security benefit. At this time, the survivor may also be eligible for the Guaranteed Income Supplement.

To find out if you are eligible and to apply for this benefit, call 1 800 277-9914 or go to www.servicecanada.gc.ca. Apply as soon as possible after the death to ensure you get the full benefits you are eligible for. You will need to supply various documents, including a copy of the death certificate.

❑ Veterans benefits

If the deceased was receiving a Veterans Affairs Disability Pension, the surviving spouse (including common-law partners) may receive, for one year, a pension equal to what the deceased was receiving at the time of death. After one year, a survivor's pension will be paid. Surviving children may be eligible for orphan benefits.

Veterans Affairs Canada may pay for some death-related expenses (such as funeral and burial) for eligible Canadian and allied veterans.

For more information, contact Veterans Affairs Canada at 1 866 522-2122 or go to www.vac-acc.gc.ca.

❑ Employer death benefits

Contact the deceased's employer to find out if there are death benefits payable to survivors.

❑ Workplace Safety and Insurance Board

If a worker dies by suicide following a work-related injury, the Workplace Safety and Insurance Board must pay benefits to the worker's dependents if it is established that the suicide resulted from the work-related injury.

For more information, call 1 800 387-0750 or go to www.wsib.on.ca.

Your estate planning

Review your personal will, power of attorney, beneficiaries and other legal and financial documents to see if you need to update them, as a result of your friend or family member's death.

4

Final words

Beyond surviving

- Know you can survive. You may not think so, but you can.
- Question why it happened until you no longer need to know why or until you are satisfied with partial answers.
- Know you may feel overwhelmed by the intensity of your feelings—and that all your feelings are normal.
- You may feel confused and forgetful. This is common when you are mourning.
- You may feel angry with the person, with the world, with God, with yourself. It's okay to express it. It is also okay not to feel angry.
- You may feel guilty for what you think you did or did not do. Let guilt turn to forgiveness of yourself and others.
- Having suicidal thoughts is common. It does not mean you will act on those thoughts. If the thoughts continue, seek help and support.
- Remember to take one moment or one day at a time.
- Find a good listener with whom to share. Call someone when you need to talk.

- Don't be afraid to cry. Tears are healing.
- Give yourself time to heal.
- Remember: The choice was not yours. No one is the sole influence in another's life.
- Expect setbacks. If emotions return like a tidal wave, you may be experiencing a remnant of grief, which is a normal part of grieving.
- Put off major decisions if you can.
- Give yourself permission to get professional help.
- Be aware of the pain of your family and friends.
- Be patient with yourself and with others who may not understand.
- Set your own limits and learn to say "No."
- Steer clear of people who want to tell you what or how to feel.
- Do not accept blame from yourself or others.
- Know that there are support groups that can be helpful. If not, ask a professional to help start one.
- Call on your personal faith and values to help you through.
- It is common to experience physical reactions to your grief, such as headaches, loss of appetite and difficulty sleeping.
- The willingness to laugh with others and at yourself is healing.
- Wear out your questions, anger, guilt or other feelings until you can let them go. Letting go doesn't mean forgetting.
- Know that you will never be the same again—and that you can survive and even go beyond surviving.

Adapted from I. Bolton & C. Mitchell. (1983). My Son...My Son: A Guide to Healing after Death, Loss or Suicide. *Atlanta, GA: Bolton Press. With permission from Iris Bolton.*

Remembering Nicholas

The following are one family's tributes to Nicholas, a son and a brother.

Oh how I long to hug my son, hear him say: "I love you. Get a life, Pen." There is such a feeling of emptiness within. I have moments of emotional pain where tears will fall without any self-control. Grieving—I am only grieving, please don't let me grieve alone. Stay with me; listen to me as I tell you my pain.

This is the time to surround myself with pictures of my son, watch a video clip of him and recall the memories in his baby book. I go up to his room and immerse myself in his belongings and the scent of his body in his clothing before it fades. I look at each picture and remember the time that relates to the photo. I remember when he went to his friend's house for the first time. There was his birthday party we surprised him with, the whole class yelling "Surprise." I made a birthday cake in the shape of a front-end loader.

Oh, son, I wish you well and no more pain. I know you never meant to hurt your father and me, or your sisters. I just never knew you were hurting so much. I will always remember you as the considerate, thoughtful, full of life, energetic, living on the edge son, brother and friend. I will not grieve sadness. I will only allow positive grieving for you because you knew not what you were doing. I will support you, love you and respect your decisions. I realize I have no influence over what happens to any one of my young adult children when they leave the house.

Nicholas, my son, when I feel sad I tell myself, "You have taken your life, not my life." I still have so much living to do. Every morning I wake up remembering what I am grateful and thankful for, and each time, it is the fact I had 20 years with you. I carried you for nine months and you were born to me. I had the pleasure of being your mother. We are your family. Thank you for this. I am grateful for all the times you made me proud to be your mom. Nicholas, I will remember you most for your thoughtfulness and the memories you have given me. The times we laughed and the times we cried and the times we disagreed because we were being unfair with the rules of dating, dances or not being able to watch *The Simpsons*. Remember the time you had to do 40 hours of community service? You volunteered to collect for the Kidney Foundation. The times you delivered the St. Thomas newspaper after school and I'd say, "Don't talk to strangers, stay out of their houses." You would reply, "It's all good, Mom, don't worry."

When I'm sad, don't leave me alone, don't walk away. I am only grieving. There are no magic words to say. It's okay when you don't know what to say.

Penny Knapp is honoured to have been the one chosen to give birth to Nicholas. She currently works with survivors of suicide loss.

My younger brother, Nicholas, died by suicide at the age of 20. A huge weight lifted when I took out the word "committed." It is such a loaded negative word. "Nicholas died by suicide" is a more accurate way of describing what happened.

It was not the Nicholas I knew that took his own life; it was a sad, hopeless Nicholas that must have been hurting so much that he thought death was his only relief. I am very saddened that at that moment I feel Nick was short-sighted and could not hear his future calling. Coping with Nicholas's loss is a continuous rollercoaster of emotions. I go from being sad to happy to taking his death personally to asking why and becoming overwhelmed with guilt. I have learned the importance of going through all the stages of grief (sometimes more than once) without judgment. Every day I remind myself to be gentle with myself. I have a strong need to feel connected with my family; not only is it important to grieve at my own pace alone, it's also important to grieve openly with my family. The first few weeks after Nick's death, my family and I were in a cocoon—a safe haven—together. The strength I got from this helped me to slowly go back into the world accepting the fact this has changed me. I'm so blessed to have a strong, supportive family by my side.

Coping with Nick's loss just isn't enough for me. I have to do something in the name of Nicholas and that is to talk openly about how suicide has affected me, my family and my hometown. I am amazed at how many people have been touched by suicide. I'm still astonished with the statistical data surrounding it and I'm saddened so many young people—especially boys—die by suicide. I have a strong passion to make this world feel safer to young people. I need to find ways to bring hope to kids and to let them know that each and every one of them is a valuable, indispensable human being that is an integral element to today's society. I began just by feeling this need for change, then by talking about it and then by reaching out for help.

I'm so thankful to everyone who reached toward me. I see a bright future and I know that Nicholas's death was not in vain. I may have physically lost my brother, but I have found him within me. I have gained perspectives, support and a vision—a vision of how our youth need to be regarded with much more respect and dignity. I hope this also brings comfort to my mourning family and hometown community. I can tell a community's sustainability by how their youth—their futures of tomorrow—are taken care of, regarded and included. I hope the initiatives our family and community are taking toward youth programming will help all young people see and feel their own value.

Marsha Knapp Dunleavy is Nicholas's older sister. She currently works in television production in Toronto.

The death of my brother isn't some event in my life I have to get over. You grieve and cope with the death of a loved one and then it becomes a part of who you are. I am a young woman who lost her brother from suicide. I will never forget that and I can only move on once I realize this event in my life and in my family's life has now become a part of who we are. But it doesn't make it easier to forget about. You need to keep on living, but not talking about it won't help you move on. I live every day with a new part of me that has changed because of this experience of losing my brother to suicide; it has made me who I am today, much stronger. I never want to forget him. My whole family wants to do whatever we can to remember him and the times we had together as a family.

We have discovered that golf is something a lot of my family members have in common. It's relaxing, outdoors, on an amazing landscape and a part of the life we had with my brother. So, what better way to remember him than to golf in his memory?

My entire family, including extended aunts, uncles, cousins and grandparents ran our 1st Annual Memorial Golf Tournament for my brother. We raised over $20,000, we spoke out, spread the word on suicide and educated families and parents about their kids and about this secret disease.

The silence needs to be broken. SAY IT OUT LOUD! Stop whispering about it, make it known that we are not ashamed. We need to share our experiences and successes so kids feel less alone and helpless. But we can't stop there. Because we are from a small town, resources for youth are scarce. We can talk about all the skills you need as a parent or child, but where can you go to get them?

During the course of the golf tournament, we made numerous contacts with people who have struggled like us and made a difference in their own towns. We are now applying their lessons, skills and experience to our own town. Currently we have a small youth drop-in centre, which is now expanding. We need to help this resource grow not only for the benefit of our community but most of all for the kids. This centre is intended to be a home where all youth can go to express themselves, be a part of something bigger—something important to them—and give them a purpose to keep on living their fullest potential. This will also give them the pride and respect they deserve, plus the responsibility and confidence to want to make a difference in their own lives. If we can change the mind of one more person who might feel alone, and helpless, it will mean the world to me and my family. I currently work at this youth centre, which we call "Centre Ice," and will only try harder to touch the lives of the youth in this community.

Thank you to all our family and friends for your continued support and motivation. We love you. Thank you to our new-found friendships for your educational inspiration and guidance. You have all helped my family and our community to always remember Nicholas.

Melanie McLeod is the middle child and four years older than Nicholas. She currently lives in Dutton, Ontario.

"Remembering Nicholas" is reprinted by permission of the Psychiatric Patient Advocate Office from *Honouring the Past, Shaping the Future: 25 Years of Progress in Mental Health Advocacy and Rights Protection* (2008).

www.rememberingnicholas.ca

5

Resources

Many resources exist to help survivors of suicide. We have included lists of counselling associations, groups and organizations, websites and books that you may find useful. Explore the options and find which ones work best for you. We do not endorse any of these: we provide options so you know what's available and can choose for yourself.

PROFESSIONAL THERAPISTS

Ask your family doctor for a referral to someone who specializes in bereavement. You can also locate therapists in Ontario through the following websites or telephone referral services.

The College of Physicians and Surgeons of Ontario

You can use this website to find a psychiatrist (a medical doctor) in Ontario.

Note: You will have to get a referral from a family physician (general practitioner) to see a psychiatrist.

www.cpso.on.ca

Ontario Psychological Association

You can use this website to find a psychologist in Ontario.

www.psych.on.ca

416 961-0069 or 1 800 268-0069

Ontario Society of Psychotherapists

You can use this website to find a psychotherapist in Ontario.

www.psychotherapyontario.com

416 923-4050

ORGANIZATIONS

Several provincial organizations offer counselling to people grieving a death, while others offer general counselling and referrals. You may also find various local groups, including some with a specific cultural, spiritual or religious focus that you might identify with.

Aboriginal Health Access Centres (Ontario)

Several communities have Aboriginal Health Access Centres for Aboriginal people seeking support. The website lists contact information for the sites in Ontario.

www.ahwsontario.ca/programs/hacc.html

Bereaved Families of Ontario

Bereaved Families of Ontario offers support groups to families who have experienced a death. The website lists contact information for many communities across Ontario.

www.bereavedfamilies.net

Kids Help Phone

Kids Help Phone offers anonymous telephone and online counselling to young people 24 hours a day. Professional counsellors provide immediate support in English and French and, through an extensive database, can refer young people to appropriate services in their communities.

1 800 668-6868

www.kidshelpphone.ca

Mental Health Service Information Ontario

Mental Health Service Information Ontario provides information about mental health services and supports in communities across Ontario.

1 866 531-2600

www.mhsio.on.ca

WEBSITES

Following are a number of websites providing more in-depth information that you may find useful.

American Association of Suicidology

The American Association of Suicidology provides information for people involved in suicide prevention and intervention and for those touched by suicide. Through this website you can subscribe to an online newsletter, *Surviving Suicide*.

www.suicidology.org

American Foundation for Suicide Prevention

This website contains numerous resources on suicide, suicide prevention and surviving suicide.

www.afsp.org

Canadian Mental Health Association

This website provides information on suicide and grief after suicide under "About Mental Health."

www.ontario.cmha.ca

Canadian Association for Suicide Prevention

This website focuses on preventing suicides and supporting people who have lost someone to suicide.

www.suicideprevention.ca

Centre for Suicide Prevention

This Canadian website is a library and resource centre providing information on suicide and suicidal behaviour. The site does not address issues related to survivors of suicide but does provide information, such as statistics, that you may find useful.

www.suicideinfo.ca

Choose Life

The Choose Life strategy and action plan focuses on prevention and early intervention for suicide in Scotland, and offers optimism for the future. The "Bereaved by Suicide" section provides a link to a booklet, *After a Suicide*, that contains similar content to *Hope and Healing*.

www.chooselife.net

The Gift of Keith

This memorial website provides a variety of resources for survivors of suicide.

http://thegiftofkeith.org

Grief after Suicide

This Canadian Mental Health Association web page discusses how grief from a suicide can be different from the grief experienced with other deaths.

www.cmha.ca/bins/content_page.asp?cid=3-101-103&lang=1

Let's Talk about Grief

New Brunswick's Department of Health developed this guide for people who have had someone close to them die by suicide.

www.gnb.ca/0055/pdf/1279e-final.pdf

National Survivors of Suicide Day

The American Foundation for Suicide Prevention (AFSP) sponsors this annual day of healing for survivors of suicide. The website lists participating cities worldwide and links you to the AFSP broadcast of the events.

www.afsp.org/index.cfm?fuseaction=home.viewPage&page_id=FEE7D778-CF08-CB44-DA1285B6BBCF366E

Ontario Association for Suicide Prevention

The "Resources" section of this website lists bereavement groups in Ontario for survivors of suicide.

www.ospn.ca

Suicide Awareness Voices of Education

The "Coping with Loss" section of this website provides information on several topics, including grieving and what to tell children.

www.save.org

The Suicide Memorial Wall

The purpose of this website is to provide a space where people can remember those who died by suicide by submitting their name for the memorial wall.

www.suicidememorialwall.com

The Suicide Paradigm

This website provides information related to suicide, suicide prevention and suicide loss.

http://lifegard.tripod.com

Survivors

This section of the Canadian website Suicide Prevention Education Awareness Knowledge provides information for survivors of suicide and offers advice for friends and family on how to listen to someone who is grieving.

www.speak-out.ca/survivors.htm

Survivors of Suicide

This website offers information for survivors of suicide and for those who are helping them heal.

www.survivorsofsuicide.com

BOOKS

Alexander, V. (1998). *In the Wake of Suicide: Stories of the People Left Behind*. San Francisco: Jossey-Bass Publishers.

Barrett, T. (1989). *Life After Suicide: The Survivor's Grief Experience*. Fargo, ND: Aftermath Research.

Baugher, B. & Jordan, J. (2002). *After Suicide Loss: Coping with Your Grief*. Newcastle, WA: R. Baugher.

Bolton, I. (with C. Mitchell. (1984). *My Son...My Son: A Guide to Healing After a Suicide in the Family*. Atlanta, GA: Bolton Press.

Carlson, T. (2000). *Suicide Survivor's Handbook: A Guide to the Bereaved and Those Who Wish to Help Them*, Expanded Edition. Duluth, MN: Benline Press.

Choy, W. (2009). *Not Yet: A Memoir Of Living And Almost Dying*. Toronto: Doubleday Canada.

Clarke, J.C. (2006). *A Mourner's Kaddish: Suicide and the Rediscovery of Hope*. Ottawa: Novalis.

Collins, J. (2007). *The Seven T's: Finding Hope and Healing in the Wake of Tragedy*. New York: Jeremy P. Tarcher/Penguin.

Davis Prend, A. (1997). *Transcending Loss: Understanding the Lifelong Impact of Grief and How to Make It Meaningful*. San Francisco: Berkley Books.

Dawson, K. (1998). *Bye Bye...I Love You*. Bermuda Dunes, CA: AfterLoss, Inc.

Dean, W. (2002). *Journaling a Pathway through Grief: One Family's Journey after the Death of a Child.* Toronto: Key Porter Books.

DeVita-Raeburn, E. (2007). *The Empty Room: Understanding Sibling Loss.* New York: Scribner.

Evans, A. (2004). *Chee Chee: A Study of Aboriginal Suicide.* Montreal: McGill-Queen's University Press.

Farr, M. (2000). *After Daniel: A Suicide Survivor's Tale.* Toronto: HarperCollins Publishers.

Fine, C. (1999). *No Time to Say Goodbye: Surviving the Suicide of a Loved One.* Mansfield, OH: Main Street Books.

Fitzgerald, H. (2000). *The Grieving Teen: A Guide for Teenagers and Their Friends.* New York: Fireside Books.

Frankel, B. & Kranz, R. (1997). *Straight Talk about Teenage Suicide.* New York: Checkmark Books.

Gewirtz, M.D. (2008). *The Gift of Grief: Finding Peace, Transformation and Renewed Life after Great Sorrow.* Berkeley, CA: Celestial Arts.

Goldman, L. (1998). *Bart Speaks Out: Breaking the Silence on Suicide.* Los Angeles, CA: Western Psychological Services.

Grollman, E.A. (1999). *Living When a Young Friend Commits Suicide...Or Even Starts Talking about It.* Boston: Beacon Press.

Hewett, J.H. (1980). *After Suicide.* Philadelphia, PA: Westminster John Knox Press.

Howe Colt, G. (2006). *November of the Soul: The Enigma of Suicide.* New York: Scribner.

Joiner, T. (2007). *Why People Die by Suicide.* Boston: Harvard University Press.

Lester, D. (Ed.). (2003). *Katie's Diary: Unlocking the Mystery of a Suicide.* New York: Routledge.

Lester, D. (1997). *The Cruelest Death: The Enigma of Adolescent Suicide.* Philadelphia: Charles Press.

Linn-Gust, M. (2002). *Do They Have Bad Days in Heaven? Surviving the Suicide Loss of a Sibling.* Albuquerque, NM: Chellehead Works.

Lukas, C. & Seiden, H.M. (1997). *Silent Grief: Living in the Wake of Suicide.* Northvale, NJ: Jason Aronson, Inc.

Mosionier, B.C. (2008). *In Search of April Raintree.* Winnipeg: Portage & Main Press.

Murphy, J.M. (1999). *Coping with Teen Suicide.* New York: Rosen Publishing Group.

Myers, M.F. & Fine, C. (2006). *Touched by Suicide: Hope and Healing after Loss.* New York: Gotham Books.

Neeld, E.H. (2003). *Seven Choices: Finding Daylight after Loss Shatters Your World.* New York: Warner Books.

Redfield Jamison, K. (2000). *Night Falls Fast: Understanding Suicide.* New York: Vintage Books.

Rubel, B. (2000). *But I Didn't Say Goodbye: For Parents and Professionals Helping Child Suicide Survivors.* Kendall Park, NJ: Griefwork Center Inc.

Sackett, J. (2005). *Goodbye Jeanine: A Mother's Faith Journey after Her Daughter's Suicide.* Colorado Springs, CO: NavPress.

Schmitt, A. (1987). *Turn Again to Life: Growing through Grief.* Scottdale, PA: Herald Press.

Schneidman, E.S. (1996). *The Suicidal Mind.* New York: Oxford University Press.

Smolin, A. & Guinan, J. (1993). *Healing after the Suicide of a Loved One.* New York: Simon & Schuster.

Staudacher, C. (1994). *A Time to Grieve: Meditations for Healing after the Death of a Loved One.* San Francisco: Harper SanFrancisco.

Stiller, B.C. (2000). *When Life Hurts: A Three-Fold Path to Healing.* Toronto: HarperCollins Canada.

Stimming, M. & Stimming, M. (Eds.). (1998). *Before Their Time: Adult Children's Experiences of Parental Suicide.* Philadelphia, PA: Temple University Press.

Tremblay, C. (2003). *Micah: A Father Survives the Suicide of His Son.* Magog, QC: Éditions Gaspe.

Van Praagh, J. (2001). *Talking to Heaven: A Medium's Message on Life After Death.* New York: Penguin Group (USA) Incorporated.

Walton, C. (2003). *When There Are No Words: Finding Your Way to Cope with Loss and Grief.* Venture, CA.: Pathfinder Publishing.

Wertheimer, A. (2001). *A Special Scar: The Experiences of People Bereaved by Suicide.* New York: Brunner-Routledge.

Westberg, G.E. (2005). *Good Grief: A Faith-Based Guide to Understanding and Healing.* Minneapolis, MN: Augsberg Books.

Willett Heavilin, M. (1988). *December's Song: Handling the Realities of Grief.* San Bernardino, CA: Here's Life.

Willett Heavilin, M. (2006). *Roses in December: Comfort for the Grieving Heart.* Eugene, OR: Harvest House Publishers.

Wolfelt, A.D. (2002). *Healing Your Traumatized Heart: 100 Practical Ideas after Someone You Love Dies a Sudden, Violent Death.* Fort Collins, CO: Companion Press.

Wolfelt, A.D. (2003). *The Journey through Grief: Reflections on Healing.* Fort Collins, CO: Companion Press.

Wolfelt, A.D. (2009). *Understanding Your Suicide Grief: Ten Essential Touchstones for Finding Hope and Healing Your Heart.* Fort Collins, CO: Companion Press.

Wright, H.N. (2004). *Experiencing Grief.* Nashville, TN: B&H Publishing Group.

Wrobleski, A. (2002). *Suicide Survivors: A Guide for Those Left Behind.* Minneapolis, MN: Afterwords.

References

Alberta Funeral Service Association. (2001). *Funerals: An Information Guide*. Retrieved from www.afsa.ab.ca/infoguide.html.

Alberta Health and Wellness. (2000). *Suicide Grief: Let's Talk About It* [pamphlet]. Alberta: Alberta Health and Wellness.

Bolton, I. & Mitchell, C. (1994). *My Son...My Son: A Guide to Healing after Death, Loss or Suicide*. Atlanta, GA: Bolton Press.

Calgary Health Region (2006). *Healing Your Spirit: Surviving after the Suicide of a Loved One*. Calgary, AB: Author.

Canadian Mental Health Association (Ontario). *Suicide Statistics*. Retrieved from www.ontario.cmha.ca/fact_sheets.asp?cID=3965.

Centre for Mental Health, NSW Health Department. (1999). *Care and Support Pack for Families and Friends Bereaved by Suicide*. New South Wales, Australia: NSW Health Department.

Chance, S. (1993, Winter). Knowing "what to expect" helps survivors cope. *Surviving Suicide*, 2–3.

Fine, C. (1997). *No Time to Say Goodbye: Surviving the Suicide of a Loved One*. New York: Doubleday.

Goldman, L. (2000, May/June). Suicide: How can we talk to the children? *The Forum Newsletter*, 1–3.

Grollman, E.A. (1988). *Suicide: Prevention, Intervention, Postvention*. Boston: Beacon Press.

Mertick, E. (1991). *Yours, Mine and Our Children's Grief: A Parent's Guide*. Alberta: Alberta Funeral Service Association.

Mertick, E. (1998). *Grieving: "Our Time"*. Alberta: Alberta Funeral Service Association.

Paraclete Video Productions (Producer). (2000). *Journey through the Shadows. Hope for Healing after Someone You Love Has Completed Suicide* [videotape].

Paraclete Video Productions (Producer). (2000). *Light amongst the Shadows. How to Help Those You Care for When Suicide Occurs* [videotape].

Province of Ontario. *What to Do When Someone Dies*. Retrieved from www.ontario.ca/en/life_events/death/004448.

Red Deer City RCMP Victim Services (2001). *Dealing with the Loss of a Loved One*. Red Deer, AB: Author.

Ross, E. (1987). *After Suicide: A Unique Grief Process*. Iowa: Lynn Publications.

Sundar, P. (2002) *Support for Supporters: A Resource Package for Providing Support to Bereaved Adolescents*. Bereaved Families of Ontario.

Supporting suicide survivors. (1999, November). *SIEC Alert, 1*.

Wrobleski, A. (1991). *Suicide: Survivors. A Guide for Those Left Behind*. Minneapolis: Afterwords.